Doc Keagan's
ZYX

Peanut Butter

Chocolate

A Division Of Hice Publishing, Inc.
Unique Learner Books

To Mom and Dad
Thank you for helping me become an author!

Tiny z

Giant Z

How many words
start with z?

Zanzabariah, a zestful zebra
zig-zags through the zenful
plains of Zambia.

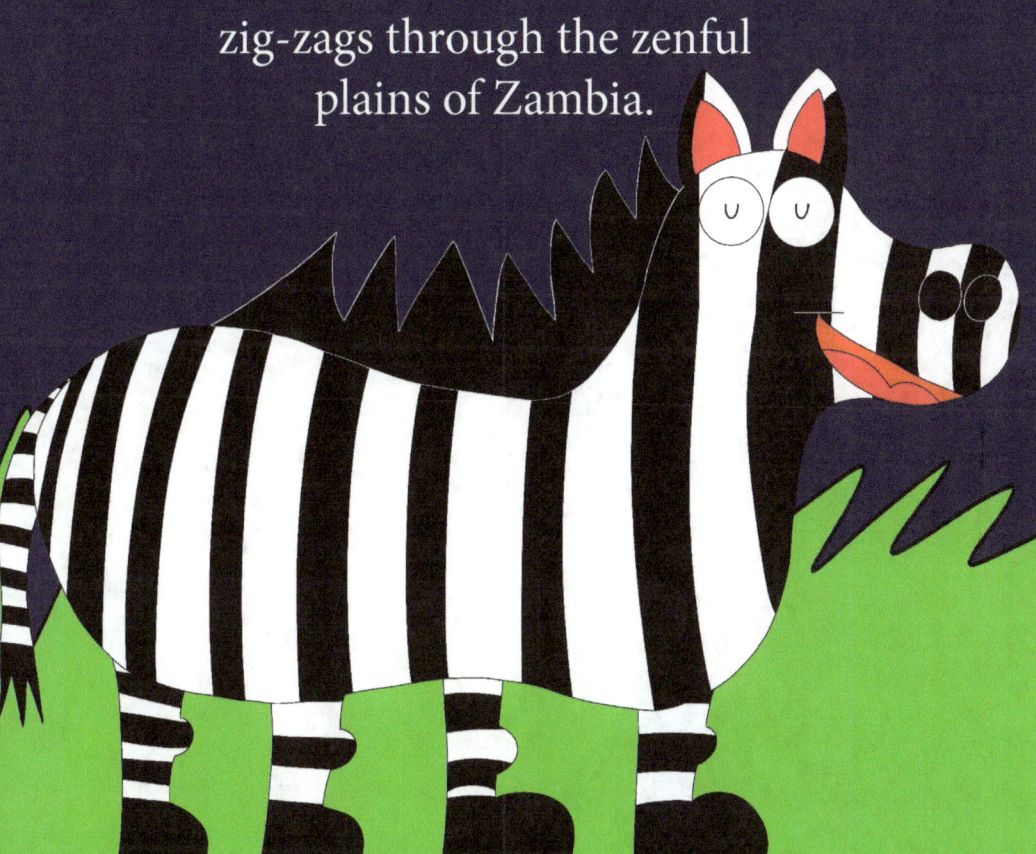

Tiny y

Giant Y

How many words
start with y?

Young people ride on a yellow yacht
yielding through the Yabbadabbadoo
Sea to Yemen for a year.

Tiny x

Giant X

How many words
start with x?

X is the uniquest letter. I rarely use it.
But here are xenodochial people
living in a xanthic, xyloyd,
and xanadu building.

Tiny w

Giant W

How many words
start with w?

Willy, a wild walrus, lives in the whimsical Wadden Sea. He waddles across white ice and wet water to his well wisher, Walter.

ZYXWV...

Various amounts of vegetable
varities in a vibrant violet
veggie box!

V...v...V

Tiny u

Giant U

How many words
start with u?

Uckle-U, the Unicorn, is a unique, unicolored, and an unusual pretend horse that I can't use!

Tom the tired tiger is tucked tightly and asleep next to the tall, teak tree in the tropical rainforest.

Tiny s

Giant S

How many words
start with s?

Simon lives in Sapporo and is starving for
salmon sushi with sashimi and soy sauce.

Tiny r

Giant R

How many words
start with r?

Red is a realistic color residing in
a romantic and radiant rainbow.

ZYXWVUTSRQ...

Quoogan, the quirky quooting quail
went on a quick quest, and said
"QUOOT!"

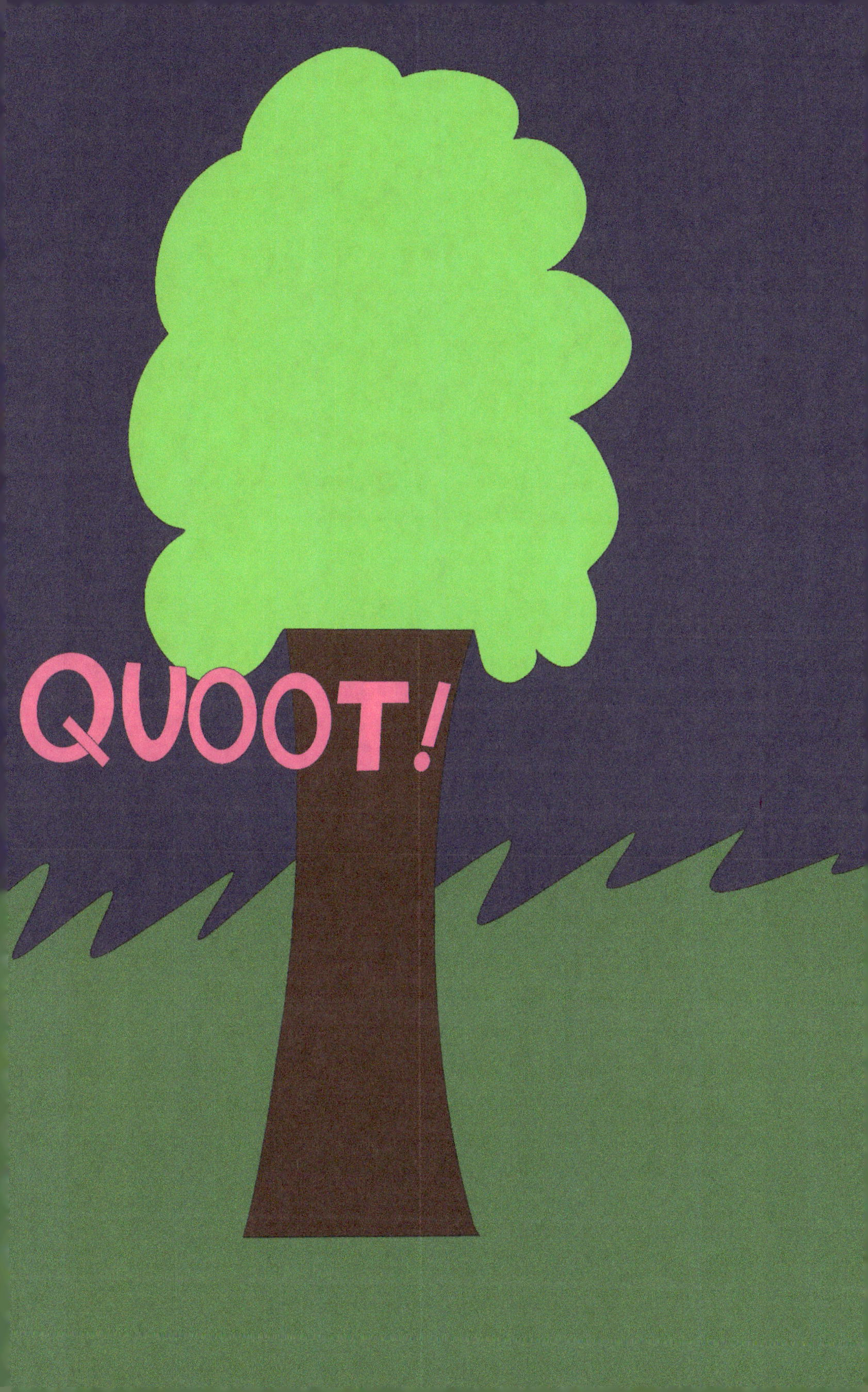
QUOOT!

Tiny p

Giant P

How many words
start with p?

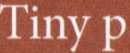

Parker, Peter, Penny, and Paula are peaceful and pleasing pals playing on a popular playground with purple stairs and a pink slide at Patterson Elementary School.

Giant O

How many words
start with o?

Olson, an odd, obscure, and oinking pig lives
in an oblong pen with odorous
mud and says, "OINK!"

Giant N

How many words
start with n?

Noah is a nimble, nice, and noisy native American who lives in New Mexico.

Tiny m

Giant M

How many words
start with m?

Mellie the moody and mischievous
monkey marvels at the many mangos on the
mango tree in Magdelena by the moonlight.

Tiny l

Giant L

How many words
start with l?

Liam the lucky, loyal, and leashed dog is
wearing a lavender leash while laying down
on the lush lawn at Laguana Beach Dog Park.

Giant K

How many words
start with k?

Kevin has a keen sense of smell
as he whiffs his koscher fries and
king-like burger with ketchup.

ZYXWVUTSR QPONMLKJ...

Jovial James looks at a jesting, jeering, and joyous jack-in-the-box on the jazzy jukebox.

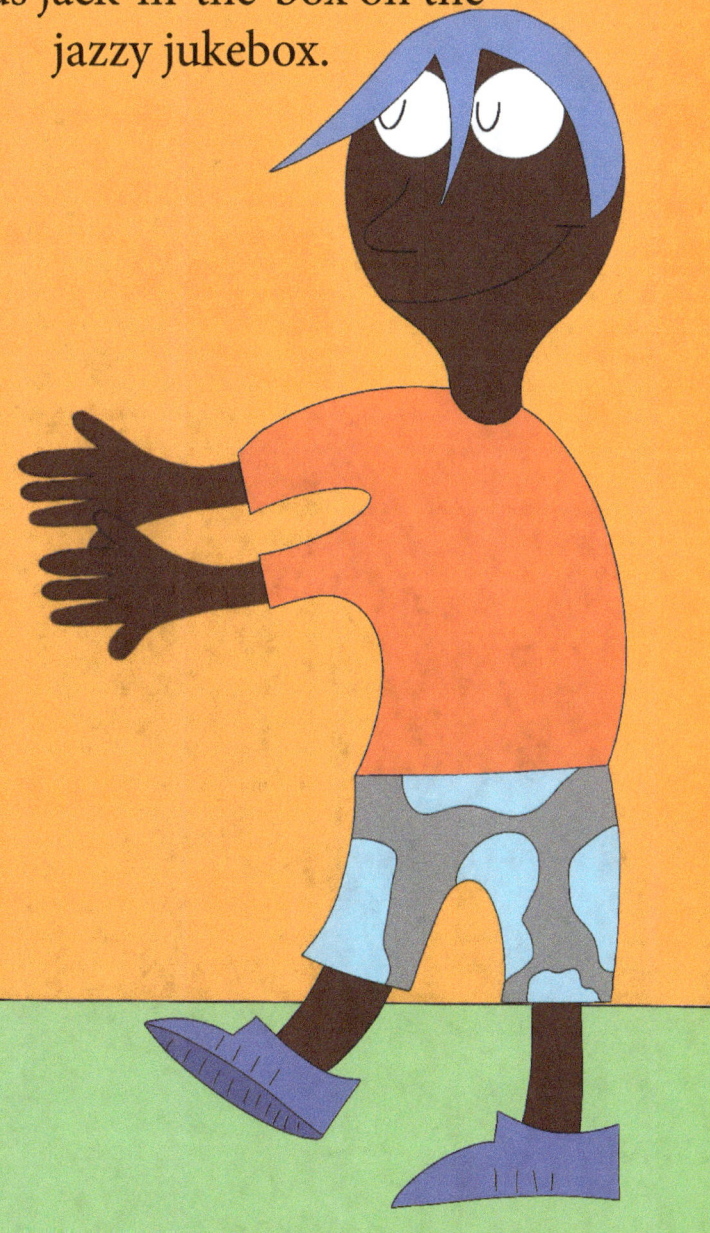

ZYXWVUTSR QPONMLKJI...

Chocolate is licking the impressively immense and irresistible, icy-ice indigo ice cream and Peanut Butter is inquistive and interested.

HOO!

Tiny h

Giant H

How many words
start with h?

Helen the huge, headstrong, hilarious,
and hooting owl is sitting on a high
healthy tree branch having leaves
and saying, "HOO!"

Tiny g

Giant G

How many words
start with g?

Grayland the glad, growing, and goofy
guinea pig is grinning on the great,
green, and gorgeous grass.

Tiny f

GIANT F

How many words
start with f?

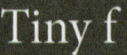

Five festive foods on a fabulous, fantastic, and a fairly full plate. A fruitful apple, a flavored carrot, fresh ham, farm-fresh cow milk, and foreign grains on a formal, fuchsia counter.

Tiny e

Giant E

How many words
start with e?

Ethlando the exciting and exemplary elf
is enjoying an exquisite Christmas Eve
with his elegant evergreen tree.

ZYXWVUTSRQP
ONMLKJIHGFED...

Dr. Doc, the delightful and dutiful doctor is in his decorative doctor's office dedicated to due diligence. "Wink! Wink!"

Tiny c

Giant C

How many words start with c?

Cam cooked crunchy corn on the cob as
Peanut Butter and Chococlate counted their
cash so they could collect their commerce.

Bertie the best, brilliant, black, yellow
and white bumblebee is busy buzzing up
buttercup flowers in the big, bright blue sky.

Tiny a

Giant A

How many words start with a?

Chocolate and Peanut Butter were astonished
at an amazing, amazon antelope
also known as an addax.